Classically Inspired Sketchbook
Public Domain Poems To Copy, Research, & Illustrate
By Eric Gibbons and Michelle Lovejoy

Copy Editing by Kim Huyler Defibaugh, Ed.D.

ISBN-13: 978-1-940290-58-4
ISBN-10: 1-940290-58-9

Published by Firehouse Publications: www.FirehousePublications.com
Printed by Createspace

Limited Copyright Agreement: The purchaser of this book, <u>whose name shall appear below</u>, is authorized by their purchase to make copies for the instruction of their students. Should multiple instructors teach from these materials, each instructor must purchase their own copy. This copyright does not extend beyond the individual to a whole department, school, or district. One copy per instructor may be copied.

If no name appears below, then the following copyright will be in force:
No part of this book may be used or reproduced by any means, graphic, electronic, or mechanical, including photocopying, recording, taping or by any information storage retrieval system without the written permission of the author except in the case of brief quotations embodied in critical articles and reviews.

Printed Name of purchaser: _____

Signature of purchaser: _____

Date of Purchase: ___/___/_____

Venue of purchase _____

Introduction

This book was created as a collaboration between an art teacher who is an author, and an English teacher who loves art. Illustration and verse have long been great partners; one cannot survive long without the other. We present these classical poems to be explored and illustrated, giving them new life. From Shakespeare to Louis Carroll and many in-between, no one should go through life without being exposed to these timeless works of poetry.

Welcome to the Public Domain

The term "public domain" refers to creative materials that are not protected by intellectual property laws such as copyright, trademark, or patent laws. The public owns these works, not an individual author or artist. Anyone can use a public domain work without obtaining permission, but no one can ever own it. An important wrinkle to understand about public domain material is that, while each work belongs to the public, collections of public domain works may be protected by copyright. If, for example, someone has collected public domain images in a book or on a website, the collection as a whole may be protectable even though individual images are not. You are free to copy and use individual images but copying and distributing the complete collection may infringe what is known as the "collective works" copyright. Collections of public domain material will be protected if the person who created it has used creativity in the choices and organization of the public domain material. This usually involves some unique selection process, for example, a poetry scholar compiling a book — The Greatest Poems of William Shakespeare.

There are four common ways that works arrive in the public domain:
- The copyright has expired
- The copyright owner failed to follow copyright renewal rules
- The copyright owner deliberately places it in the public domain, as a "dedication"
- Copyright law does not protect this type of work

A Note For Teachers

This book is set up so that you may make copies for your students as a regular assignment or potential substitute plan. I encourage you to have students translate or summarize poems before creating illustrations as this helps them more deeply explore the topic. Some poems are longer than others. It might be better to have them choose, or you might assign a specific stanza or portion to summarize. If each stanza is assigned to a different student or groups of students, at the end the whole poem can be displayed with illustrations, showing off the awesome inter-curricular work you do.

CONTENTS

- 4 — "The Jabberwocky" by Lewis Carroll
- 8 — "The Road Not Taken" by Robert Frost
- 12 — "Mending Wall" by Robert Frost
- 16 — "O Captain! My Captain!" by Walt Whitman
- 20 — "The Deserted House" by Alfred Lord Tennyson
- 24 — "Crossing the Bar" by Alfred Lord Tennyson
- 28 — "The Garden of Love" by William Blake
- 32 — "The Tiger" by William Blake
- 36 — "A Poison Tree" by William Blake
- 40 — "I Wandered Lonely as a Cloud" by William Wordsworth
- 44 — "Sonnet 18" by William Shakespeare
- 48 — "Sonnet 29" by William Shakespeare
- 52 — "Casey At The Bat" by Ernest L. Thayer
- 57 — "The Raven" by Edgar Allan Poe
- 62 — "Life" by Charlotte Brontë
- 66 — "Sonnet XLIII" by Elizabeth Barrett Browning
- 70 — "We Wear The Mask" by Paul Laurence Dunbar
- 74 — "On The Bridge" by Kate Greenaway
- 78 — "Trees" by Alfred Joyce Kilmer
- 82 — "Roofs" by Alfred Joyce Kilmer
- 86 — "City Trees" by Edna St. Vincent Millay
- 90 — "As Long As Your Eyes Are Blue" by Banjo Paterson (Andrew Barton)
- 94 — "Song" by Christina Georgina Rossetti
- 98 — "Miniver Cheevy" by Edwin Arlington Robinson
- 102 — "The Knight's Song" by Lewis Carroll
- 106 — "Lady Icicle" by Emily Pauline Johnson
- 110 — "Jack And Jill" by Clara Doty Bates
- 114 — "Annabel Lee" by Edgar Allan Poe
- 118 — "My Boy" by Morris Rosenfeld
- 122 — "Fairy Song" by Louisa May Alcott
- 126 — "The Ultimate Joy" by an unknown author
- 130 — "Marriage Fees" by an unknown author
- 134 — "Two Fishers" by an unknown author

"The Jabberwocky" by Lewis Carroll

`Twas brillig, and the slithy toves
Did gyre and gimble in the wabe:
All mimsy were the borogoves,
And the mome raths outgrabe.

"Beware the Jabberwock, my son!
The jaws that bite, the claws that catch!
Beware the Jubjub bird, and shun
The frumious Bandersnatch!"

He took his vorpal sword in hand:
Long time the manxome foe he sought--
So rested he by the Tumtum tree,
And stood awhile in thought.

And, as in uffish thought he stood,
The Jabberwock, with eyes of flame,
Came whiffling through the tulgey wood,
And burbled as it came!

One, two! One, two! And through and through
The vorpal blade went snicker-snack!
He left it dead, and with its head
He went galumphing back.

"And, has thou slain the Jabberwock?
Come to my arms, my beamish boy!
O frabjous day! Callooh! Callay!"
He chortled in his joy.

`Twas brillig, and the slithy toves
Did gyre and gimble in the wabe;
All mimsy were the borogoves,
And the mome raths outgrabe.

Analyze the Poem:

This poem is a story. Each stanza tells a part of the story but the language is very unusual. What happened in this unusual poem?

The first stanza sets the tone for the poem. It gives a sense of the place where this story happens. Hardly any of the words are real, but when you say them they "feel" like a special kind of place. What do you feel the environment looks like? Desert, swamp, forest, jungle, hot, cold, wet? How would you describe it?

_____

_____

_____

The next 5 stanzas tell a story. Write what happened in each one.

1 _____

_____

2 _____

_____

3 _____

_____

4 _____

_____

5 _____

_____

What specific details do you know about the Jabberwocky and the way it looks and moves?

_____

_____

_____

Create a drawing on the next page based on the stanza your teacher has assigned or your favorite one. Include some of the text in a creative way.

Extended Exploration:

Write a short synopsis of the poem. What main idea or story was told?

_____

_____

_____

_____

_____

Lewis Carroll was born Charles Lutwidge Dodgson on January 27, 1832 and died January 14, 1898. He was an English writer, mathematician, logician, Anglican deacon, and photographer. His most famous writings are *Alice's Adventures in Wonderland* and its sequel *Through the Looking-Glass*. The latter includes the poem *Jabberwocky* and is an example of the genre of literary nonsense. Carroll is noted for his facility at word play, logic and fantasy.

Discover or research 5 more facts about the author or poem.

1 _____

_____

2 _____

_____

3 _____

_____

4 _____

_____

5 _____

_____

"The Road Not Taken" by Robert Frost

Two roads diverged in a yellow wood,
And sorry I could not travel both
And be one traveler, long I stood
And looked down one as far as I could
To where it bent in the undergrowth;

Then took the other, as just as fair,
And having perhaps the better claim,
Because it was grassy and wanted wear;
Though as for that the passing there
Had worn them really about the same,

And both that morning equally lay
In leaves no step had trodden black.
Oh, I kept the first for another day!
Yet knowing how way leads on to way,
I doubted if I should ever come back.

I shall be telling this with a sigh
Somewhere ages and ages hence:
Two roads diverged in a wood, and I—
I took the one less traveled by,
And that has made all the difference.

Analyze the Poem:

This short poem has four stanzas. Write the main idea from each stanza below.

1 _____

_____

2 _____

_____

3 _____

_____

4 _____

_____

An allegory is a story, poem, or picture that can be interpreted to reveal a hidden meaning, usually a moral or political one. What might be the hidden message of this poem?

_____

_____

_____

_____

_____

_____

On the next page create a drawing around the text of the poem to help illustrate the meaning.

"The Road Not Taken"
by Robert Frost

Two roads diverged in a yellow wood,
And sorry I could not travel both
And be one traveler, long I stood
And looked down one as far as I could
To where it bent in the undergrowth;

Then took the other, as just as fair,
And having perhaps the better claim,
Because it was grassy and wanted wear;
Though as for that the passing there
Had worn them really about the same,

And both that morning equally lay
In leaves no step had trodden black.
Oh, I kept the first for another day!
Yet knowing how way leads on to way,
I doubted if I should ever come back.

I shall be telling this with a sigh
Somewhere ages and ages hence:
Two roads diverged in a wood, and I—
I took the one less traveled by,
And that has made all the difference.

Extended Exploration:

Write a short synopsis of the poem. What main idea or story was told?

_____

_____

_____

_____

_____

Robert Frost was born on March 26, 1874 and died January 29, 1963. An American poet, his work was published in England before it was published in America. In his writings, Frost frequently used settings from early twentieth century rural life in New England as a vehicle to examine social and philosophical themes. He received four Pulitzer Prizes for Poetry and was awarded the Congressional Gold Medal in 1960 for his poetic works. Frost was named poet laureate of Vermont.

Discover or research 5 more facts about the author or poem.

1 _____

_____

2 _____

_____

3 _____

_____

4 _____

_____

5 _____

_____

"Mending Wall" by Robert Frost

Something there is that doesn't love a wall,
That sends the frozen-ground-swell under it,
And spills the upper boulders in the sun;
And makes gaps even two can pass abreast.
The work of hunters is another thing:
I have come after them and made repair
Where they have left not one stone on a stone,
But they would have the rabbit out of hiding,
To please the yelping dogs. The gaps I mean,
No one has seen them made or heard them made,
But at spring mending-time we find them there.
I let my neighbor know beyond the hill;
And on a day we meet to walk the line
And set the wall between us once again.
We keep the wall between us as we go.
To each the boulders that have fallen to each.
And some are loaves and some so nearly balls
We have to use a spell to make them balance:
"Stay where you are until our backs are turned!"
We wear our fingers rough with handling them.
Oh, just another kind of out-door game,
One on a side. It comes to little more:
There where it is we do not need the wall:
He is all pine and I am apple orchard.
My apple trees will never get across
And eat the cones under his pines, I tell him.
He only says, "Good fences make good neighbors."
Spring is the mischief in me, and I wonder
If I could put a notion in his head:
"Why do they make good neighbors? Isn't it
Where there are cows? But here there are no cows.
Before I built a wall I'd ask to know
What I was walling in or walling out,
And to whom I was like to give offence.
Something there is that doesn't love a wall,
That wants it down." I could say "Elves" to him,
But it's not elves exactly, and I'd rather
He said it for himself. I see him there
Bringing a stone grasped firmly by the top
In each hand, like an old-stone savage armed.
He moves in darkness as it seems to me,
Not of woods only and the shade of trees.
He will not go behind his father's saying,
And he likes having thought of it so well
He says again, "Good fences make good neighbors."

Analyze the Poem:

This poem is about a wall; it looks like a wall of text. That makes it a little hard to read but may be part of why he wrote it this way. Write 5 main ideas or things you understand from reading this poem.

1 _____

_____

2 _____

_____

3 _____

_____

4 _____

_____

5 _____

_____

An allegory is a story, poem, or picture that can be interpreted to reveal a hidden meaning, usually a moral or political one. What might be the message of this poem?

_____

_____

_____

_____

_____

On the next page create a drawing to help illustrate this poem. You may think of it as a whole or choose to focus on one part. Include some of the text in a creative way.

Extended Exploration:

Write a short synopsis of the poem. What main idea or story was told?

_____

_____

_____

_____

_____

Robert Frost was born on March 26, 1874 and died January 29, 1963. An American poet, his work was published in England before it was published in America. In his writings, Frost frequently used settings from early twentieth century rural life in New England as a vehicle to examine social and philosophical themes. He received four Pulitzer Prizes for Poetry and was awarded the Congressional Gold Medal in 1960 for his poetic works. Frost was named poet laureate of Vermont.

Discover or research 5 more facts about the author or poem.

1 _____

_____

2 _____

_____

3 _____

_____

4 _____

_____

5 _____

_____

"O Captain! My Captain!" by Walt Whitman

O Captain! My Captain! Our fearful trip is done,
The ship has weather'd every rack, the prize we sought is won,
The port is near, the bells I hear, the people all exulting,
While follow eyes the steady keel, the vessel grim and daring;
But O heart! heart! heart!
O the bleeding drops of red,
Where on the deck my Captain lies,
Fallen cold and dead.

O Captain! my Captain! rise up and hear the bells;
Rise up--for you the flag is flung--for you the bugle trills,
For you bouquets and ribbon'd wreaths--for you the shores a-crowding,
For you they call, the swaying mass, their eager faces turning;
Here Captain! dear father!
This arm beneath your head!
It is some dream that on the deck,
You've fallen cold and dead.

My Captain does not answer, his lips are pale and still,
My father does not feel my arm, he has no pulse nor will,
The ship is anchor'd safe and sound, its voyage closed and done,
From fearful trip the victor ship comes in with object won;
Exult O shores, and ring O bells!
But I with mournful tread,
Walk the deck my Captain lies,
Fallen cold and dead.

Analyze the Poem:

This short poem has three stanzas. Write the main idea from each below.

1 _____

_____

_____

2 _____

_____

_____

3 _____

_____

_____

Illustrations help tell a story. What things can you draw to help illustrate this poem?

_____

_____

_____

_____

_____

On the next page create a drawing to help illustrate this poem. You may think of it as a whole or choose to focus on one part. Include some of the text in a creative way.

Extended Exploration:

Write a short synopsis of the poem. What main idea or story was told?

_____

_____

_____

_____

_____

Walter "Walt" Whitman was born on May 31, 1819 and died on March 26, 1892. An American poet, essayist, and journalist, Whitman is among the most influential poets in the American style. Often called the father of free verse (poetry that does not have rhyme or have a regular meter), Whitman worked as a journalist, teacher, government clerk, and was a volunteer nurse during he American Civil War. tWhitman's major work, *Leaves of Grass*, was an attempt at reaching out to the common person with an American epic. He continued expanding and revising it until his death in 1892.

Discover or research 5 more facts about the author or poem.

1 _____

_____

2 _____

_____

3 _____

_____

4 _____

_____

5 _____

_____

"The Deserted House" by Alfred Lord Tennyson

Life and Thought have gone away
Side by side,
Leaving door and windows wide:
Careless tenants they!

All within is dark as night:
In the windows is no light;
And no murmur at the door,
So frequent on its hinge before.

Close the door, the shutters close,
Or thro' the windows we shall see
The nakedness and vacancy
Of the dark deserted house.
Come away: no more of mirth
Is here or merry-making sound.
The house was builded of the earth,
And shall fall again to ground.

Come away: for Life and Thought
Here no longer dwell;
But in a city glorious--
A great and distant city--have bought
A mansion incorruptible.
Would they could have stayed with us!

Analyze the Poem:

This short poem has four stanzas. Write the main idea or what you understand from each below.

1 _____

_____

2 _____

_____

3 _____

_____

4 _____

_____

An allegory is a story, poem, or picture that can be interpreted to reveal a hidden meaning, usually a moral or political one. What might be the hidden message of this poem?

_____

_____

_____

_____

_____

On the next page create a drawing around the text of the poem to help illustrate the meaning.

"The Deserted House"
by Alfred Lord Tennyson

Life and Thought have gone away
Side by side,
Leaving door and windows wide:
Careless tenants they!

All within is dark as night:
In the windows is no light;
And no murmur at the door,
So frequent on its hinge before.

Close the door, the shutters close,
Or thro' the windows we shall see
The nakedness and vacancy
Of the dark deserted house.
Come away: no more of mirth
Is here or merry-making sound.
The house was builded of the earth,
And shall fall again to ground.

Come away: for Life and Thought
Here no longer dwell;
But in a city glorious--
A great and distant city--have bought
A mansion incorruptible.
Would they could have stayed with us!

Extended Exploration:

Write a short synopsis of the poem. What main idea or story was told?

_____

_____

_____

_____

_____

Alfred Tennyson, 1st Baron Tennyson, was born on 6 August 1809 and died 6 on October 1892. He was Poet Laureate of Great Britain and Ireland during much of Queen Victoria's reign and remains one of the most popular British poets. Much of his writing was based on classical mythological themes, such as Ulysses. During his career, Tennyson attempted drama but his plays had little success. He was famous for many sayings, this in particular: "Tis better to have loved and lost – Than never to have loved at all."

Discover or research 5 more facts about the author or poem.

1 _____

_____

2 _____

_____

3 _____

_____

4 _____

_____

5 _____

_____

"Crossing the Bar" by Alfred Lord Tennyson

Sunset and evening star,
And one clear call for me!
And may there be no moaning of the bar,
When I put out to sea,

But such a tide as moving seems asleep,
Too full for sound and foam,
When that which drew from out the boundless deep
Turns again home.

Twilight and evening bell,
And after that the dark!
And may there be no sadness of farewell,
When I embark;

For though from out our bourne of Time and Place
The flood may bear me far,
I hope to see my Pilot face to face
When I have crossed the bar.

Analyze the Poem:

This short poem has four stanzas. Write the main idea from each below.

1 _____

_____

2 _____

_____

3 _____

_____

4 _____

_____

An allegory is a story, poem, or picture that can be interpreted to reveal a hidden meaning. This poem describes the sunset and coming of the evening star as well as darkness. The "bar" is a sand bar, a shallow area one passes before going out to sea. Describe how the poet seems to feel about this time before sunset. Illustrate it on the next page.

_____

_____

_____

_____

_____

On the next page create a drawing around the text of the poem to help illustrate the meaning.

"Crossing the Bar"
by Alfred Lord Tennyson

Sunset and evening star,
And one clear call for me!
And may there be no moaning of the bar,
When I put out to sea,

But such a tide as moving seems asleep,
Too full for sound and foam,
When that which drew from out the boundless deep
Turns again home.

Twilight and evening bell,
And after that the dark!
And may there be no sadness of farewell,
When I embark;

For though from out our bourne of Time and Place
The flood may bear me far,
I hope to see my Pilot face to face
When I have crossed the bar.

Extended Exploration:

Write a short synopsis of the poem. What main idea or story was told?

_____

_____

_____

_____

_____

_____

Alfred Tennyson, 1st Baron Tennyson, was born on 6 August 1809 and died 6 on October 1892. He was Poet Laureate of Great Britain and Ireland during much of Queen Victoria's reign and remains one of the most popular British poets. Much of his writing was based on classical mythological themes, such as Ulysses. During his career, Tennyson attempted drama but his plays had little success. He was famous for many sayings, this in particular: "Tis better to have loved and lost – Than never to have loved at all."

Discover or research 5 more facts about the author or poem.

1 _____

_____

2 _____

_____

3 _____

_____

4 _____

_____

5 _____

_____

"The Garden of Love" by William Blake

I laid me down upon a bank,
Where Love lay sleeping;
I heard among the rushes dank
Weeping, weeping.

Then I went to the heath and the wild,
To the thistles and thorns of the waste;
And they told me how they were beguiled,
Driven out, and compelled to the chaste.

I went to the Garden of Love,
And saw what I never had seen;
A Chapel was built in the midst,
Where I used to play on the green.

And the gates of this Chapel were shut
And "Thou shalt not," writ over the door;
So I turned to the Garden of Love
That so many sweet flowers bore.

And I saw it was filled with graves,
And tombstones where flowers should be;
And priests in black gowns were walking their rounds,
And binding with briars my joys and desires.

Analyze the Poem:

This short poem has five stanzas. Write the main idea or what you understand from each below.

1 _____

_____

2 _____

_____

3 _____

_____

4 _____

_____

5 _____

_____

An allegory is a story, poem, or picture that can be interpreted to reveal a hidden meaning. This poem seems particularly sad. What do you think William Blake writing about?

_____

_____

_____

_____

_____

On the next page create a drawing around the text of the poem to help illustrate the meaning.

"The Garden of Love"
by William Blake

I laid me down upon a bank,
Where Love lay sleeping;
I heard among the rushes dank
Weeping, weeping.

Then I went to the heath and the wild,
To the thistles and thorns of the waste;
And they told me how they were beguiled,
Driven out, and compelled to the chaste.

I went to the Garden of Love,
And saw what I never had seen;
A Chapel was built in the midst,
Where I used to play on the green.

And the gates of this Chapel were shut
And "Thou shalt not," writ over the door;
So I turned to the Garden of Love
That so many sweet flowers bore.

And I saw it was filled with graves,
And tombstones where flowers should be;
And priests in black gowns were walking their rounds,
And binding with briars my joys and desires.

Extended Exploration:

Write a short synopsis of the poem. What main idea or story was told?

_____

_____

_____

_____

_____

_____

William Blake was born on November 28, 1757 and died on August 12, 1827. He was an English poet, painter, and printmaker. Largely unrecognized during his lifetime, Blake is now considered a seminal figure in the history of poetry and visual arts during the Romantic Age. His visual artistry led one contemporary art critic to proclaim him "far and away the greatest artist Britain has ever produced." In 2002, Blake was placed at number 38 in the BBC's poll of the 100 Greatest Britons.

Discover or research 5 more facts about the author or poem.

1 _____

_____

2 _____

_____

3 _____

_____

4 _____

_____

5 _____

_____

"The Tiger" by William Blake

Tiger! Tiger! burning bright
In the forests of the night,
What immortal hand or eye
Could frame thy fearful symmetry?

In what distant deeps or skies
Burnt the fire of thine eyes?
On what wings dare he aspire?
What the hand dare seize the fire?

And what shoulder, and what art,
Could twist the sinews of thy heart?
And when thy heart began to beat,
What dread hand? and what dread feet?

What the hammer? what the chain?
In what furnace was thy brain?
What the anvil? what dread grasp
Dare its deadly terrors clasp?

When the stars threw down their spears,
And water'd heaven with their tears,
Did he smile his work to see?
Did he who made the Lamb make thee?

Tiger! Tiger! burning bright
In the forests of the night,
What immortal hand or eye,
Dare frame thy fearful symmetry?

Analyze the Poem:

This short poem has five unique stanzas. Write what you understand from each below.

1 _____

_____

2 _____

_____

3 _____

_____

4 _____

_____

5 _____

_____

(The 6th stanza is a repetition of the first)

This poem examines both the beauty and danger of a tiger, and questions why something so beautiful can also be terrifying. What is something you have experienced that can be both good and bad at the same time? In your answer, please use details to explain how it is both good and bad.

_____

_____

_____

_____

_____

On the next page create a drawing around the text of the poem to help illustrate the meaning.

"The Tiger" by William Blake

Tiger! Tiger! burning bright
In the forests of the night,
What immortal hand or eye
Could frame thy fearful symmetry?

In what distant deeps or skies
Burnt the fire of thine eyes?
On what wings dare he aspire?
What the hand dare seize the fire?

And what shoulder, and what art,
Could twist the sinews of thy heart?
And when thy heart began to beat,
What dread hand? and what dread feet?

What the hammer? what the chain?
In what furnace was thy brain?
What the anvil? what dread grasp
Dare its deadly terrors clasp?

When the stars threw down their spears,
And water'd heaven with their tears,
Did he smile his work to see?
Did he who made the Lamb make thee?

Tiger! Tiger! burning bright
In the forests of the night,
What immortal hand or eye,
Dare frame thy fearful symmetry?

Extended Exploration:

Write a short synopsis of the poem. What main idea or story was told?

_____

_____

_____

_____

_____

William Blake was born on November 28, 1757 and died on August 12, 1827. He was an English poet, painter, and printmaker. Largely unrecognized during his lifetime, Blake is now considered a seminal figure in the history of poetry and visual arts during the Romantic Age. His visual artistry led one contemporary art critic to proclaim him "far and away the greatest artist Britain has ever produced." In 2002, Blake was placed at number 38 in the BBC's poll of the 100 Greatest Britons.

Discover or research 5 more facts about the author or poem.

1 _____

_____

2 _____

_____

3 _____

_____

4 _____

_____

5 _____

_____

"A Poison Tree" by William Blake

I was angry with my friend:
I told my wrath, my wrath did end.
I was angry with my foe:
I told it not, my wrath did grow.

And I watered it in fears
Night and morning with my tears,
And I sunned it with smiles
And with soft deceitful wiles.

And it grew both day and night,
Till it bore an apple bright,
And my foe beheld it shine,
and he knew that it was mine,

And into my garden stole
When the night had veiled the pole;
In the morning, glad, I see
My foe outstretched beneath the tree.

Analyze the Poem:

This short poem has four stanzas. Write what you understand from each below.

1 _____

_____

2 _____

_____

3 _____

_____

4 _____

_____

William Blake was known for his dark subjects. This poem speaks of murder but does not exactly say what happened or how. Pretend you are a detective; explain the murder and how it happened. Use evidence from the poem in your answer.

_____

_____

_____

_____

_____

_____

_____

_____

On the next page create a drawing around the text of the poem to help illustrate the meaning.

"A Poison Tree" by William Blake

I was angry with my friend:
I told my wrath, my wrath did end.
I was angry with my foe:
I told it not, my wrath did grow.

And I watered it in fears
Night and morning with my tears,
And I sunned it with smiles
And with soft deceitful wiles.

And it grew both day and night,
Till it bore an apple bright,
And my foe beheld it shine,
and he knew that it was mine,

And into my garden stole
When the night had veiled the pole;
In the morning, glad, I see
My foe outstretched beneath the tree.

Extended Exploration:

Write a short synopsis of the poem. What main idea or story was told?

_____

_____

_____

_____

_____

William Blake was born on November 28, 1757 and died on August 12, 1827. He was an English poet, painter, and printmaker. Largely unrecognized during his lifetime, Blake is now considered a seminal figure in the history of poetry and visual arts during the Romantic Age. His visual artistry led one contemporary art critic to proclaim him "far and away the greatest artist Britain has ever produced." In 2002, Blake was placed at number 38 in the BBC's poll of the 100 Greatest Britons.

Discover or research 5 more facts about the author or poem.

1 _____

_____

2 _____

_____

3 _____

_____

4 _____

_____

5 _____

_____

"I Wandered Lonely as a Cloud" by William Wordsworth

I wandered lonely as a cloud
That floats on high o'er vales and hills,
When all at once I saw a crowd,
A host, of golden daffodils;
Beside the lake, beneath the trees,
Fluttering and dancing in the breeze.

Continuous as the stars that shine
And twinkle on the milky way,
They stretched in never-ending line
Along the margin of a bay:
Ten thousand saw I at a glance,
Tossing their heads in sprightly dance.

The waves beside them danced; but they
Out-did the sparkling waves in glee:
A poet could not but be gay, *(happy)*
In such a jocund company:
I gazed—and gazed—but little thought
What wealth the show to me had brought:

For oft, when on my couch I lie
In vacant or in pensive mood,
They flash upon that inward eye
Which is the bliss of solitude;
And then my heart with pleasure fills,
And dances with the daffodils.

Analyze the Poem:

This short poem has four stanzas. Write the main idea from each below.

1 _____

_____

2 _____

_____

3 _____

_____

4 _____

_____

Wordsworth uses the phrase "They flash upon that inward eye," which is interpreted to mean he's remembering something. What is he is remembering through this poem? What is a pleasant memory you can share?

_____

_____

_____

_____

_____

_____

On the next page create a drawing around the text of the poem to help illustrate the meaning.

"I Wandered Lonely as a Cloud"
by William Wordsworth

I wandered lonely as a cloud
That floats on high o'er vales and hills,
When all at once I saw a crowd,
A host, of golden daffodils;
Beside the lake, beneath the trees,
Fluttering and dancing in the breeze.

Continuous as the stars that shine
And twinkle on the milky way,
They stretched in never-ending line
Along the margin of a bay:
Ten thousand saw I at a glance,
Tossing their heads in sprightly dance.

The waves beside them danced; but they
Out-did the sparkling waves in glee:
A poet could not but be gay,
In such a jocund company:
I gazed—and gazed—but little thought
What wealth the show to me had brought:

For oft, when on my couch I lie
In vacant or in pensive mood,
They flash upon that inward eye
Which is the bliss of solitude;
And then my heart with pleasure fills,
And dances with the daffodils.

Extended Exploration:

Write a short synopsis of the poem. What main idea or story was told?

_____

_____

_____

_____

_____

William Wordsworth was born on April 7, 1770 and died on April 23, 1850. He was a major English Romantic poet who helped launch the Romantic Age in English literature with the publication Lyrical Ballads in 1798. Wordsworth's most famous work is known as "the poem to Coleridge." Wordsworth was Britain's Poet Laureate from 1843 until his death from pleurisy.

Discover or research 5 more facts about the author or poem.

1 _____

_____

2 _____

_____

3 _____

_____

4 _____

_____

5 _____

_____

"Sonnet 18" by William Shakespeare

Shall I compare thee to a summer's day?
Thou art more lovely and more temperate:
Rough winds do shake the darling buds of May,
and summer's lease hath all too short a date:

Sometimes too hot the eye of heaven shines
And often is his gold complexion dimmed;
And every fair from fair sometime declines,
By chance or nature's changing course untrimmed;

But thy eternal summer shall not fade
Nor lose possession of that fair thou owest;
Nor shall Death brag thou wanderest in his shade,
When in eternal lines to time thou growest:

So long as men can breathe or eyes can see,
So long lives this and this gives life to thee.

Analyze the Poem:

This poem is written in an older form of English, but most of it is understandable. Shakespeare's love poem compares the one he loves with a summer's day. Write five comparisons he uses below. (There are more than five to choose from.)

1 _____

_____

2 _____

_____

3 _____

_____

4 _____

_____

5 _____

_____

Explain why you think comparing someone you love to a summer's day is a good or poor comparison.

_____

_____

_____

_____

Create a drawing on the next page based Shakespeare's idea of love. Draw around the poem.

"Sonnet 18"

by William Shakespeare

Shall I compare thee to a summer's day?
Thou art more lovely and more temperate:
Rough winds do shake the darling buds of May,
and summer's lease hath all too short a date:
Sometimes too hot the eye of heaven shines
And often is his gold complexion dimmed;
And every fair from fair sometime declines,
By chance or nature's changing course untrimmed;
But thy eternal summer shall not fade
Nor lose possession of that fair thou owest;
Nor shall Death brag thou wanderest in his shade,
When in eternal lines to time thou growest:
   So long as men can breathe or eyes can see,
   So long lives this and this gives life to thee.

Extended Exploration:

Write a short synopsis of the poem. What main idea or story was told?

_____

_____

_____

_____

_____

William Shakespeare has an unknown birthdate but we know he was baptized April 26, 1564 and died April 23, 1616. He was an English poet, playwright, and actor. Widely regarded as the greatest writer in the English language and the world's best dramatist, he is often called England's national poet and the "Bard of Avon." His works, including collaborations, consist of approximately 38 plays, 154 sonnets, two long narrative poems, and a few other verses. His plays have been translated into every major living language and are performed more often than those of any other playwright.

Discover or research 5 more facts about the author or poem.

1 _____

_____

2 _____

_____

3 _____

_____

4 _____

_____

5 _____

_____

"Sonnet 29" by William Shakespeare

When in disgrace with fortune and men's eyes
I all alone beweep my outcast state,
And trouble deaf heaven with my bootless cries,
And look upon myself, and curse my fate,

Wishing me like to one more rich in hope,
Featur'd like him, like him with friends possess'd,
Desiring this man's art, and that man's scope,
With what I most enjoy contented least;

Yet in these thoughts my self almost despising,
Haply I think on thee, and then my state,
Like to the lark at break of day arising
From sullen earth, sings hymns at heaven's gate,

For thy sweet love remember'd such wealth brings
That then I scorn to change my state with kings.

Analyze the Poem:

This poem is written in an older form of English, but most of it is understandable. Shakespeare's poem starts out sad but ends with hope. He wrote this poem as one paragraph but we have divided it into 4 parts to make it easier to read and understand. Write what you understand from each of the four stanzas.

1 _____

_____

2 _____

_____

3 _____

_____

4 _____

_____

Shakespeare is describing a time when he was very unhappy but a memory helps bring him out of his depression. We have all faced times that were difficult, and found hope somehow. Describe a time when you felt sad or depressed and what helped you through it.

_____
_____
_____
_____
_____
_____
_____

Create a drawing on the next page based Shakespeare's poem. Draw around the poem.

"Sonnet 29"
by William Shakespeare

When in disgrace with fortune and men's eyes
I all alone beweep my outcast state,
And trouble deaf heaven with my bootless cries,
And look upon myself, and curse my fate,
Wishing me like to one more rich in hope,
Featur'd like him, like him with friends possess'd,
Desiring this man's art, and that man's scope,
With what I most enjoy contented least;
Yet in these thoughts my self almost despising,
Haply I think on thee, and then my state,
Like to the lark at break of day arising
From sullen earth, sings hymns at heaven's gate,
   For thy sweet love remember'd such wealth brings
   That then I scorn to change my state with kings.

Extended Exploration:

Write a short synopsis of the poem. What main idea or story was told?

_____

_____

_____

_____

_____

William Shakespeare has an unknown birthdate but we know he was baptized April 26, 1564 and died April 23, 1616. He was an English poet, playwright, and actor. Widely regarded as the greatest writer in the English language and the world's best dramatist, he is often called England's national poet and the "Bard of Avon." His works, including collaborations, consist of approximately 38 plays, 154 sonnets, two long narrative poems, and a few other verses. His plays have been translated into every major living language and are performed more often than those of any other playwright.

Discover or research 5 more facts about the author or poem.

1 _____

_____

2 _____

_____

3 _____

_____

4 _____

_____

5 _____

_____

"Casey At The Bat" by Ernest L. Thayer

The outlook wasn't brilliant for the Mudville Nine that day;
the score stood four to two, with but one inning more to play.
And then when Cooney died at first, and Barrows did the same,
a sickly silence fell upon the patrons of the game.

A straggling few got up to go in deep despair. The rest
clung to that hope which springs eternal in the human breast;
they thought, if only Casey could get but a whack at that –
they'd put up even money, now, with Casey at the bat.

But Flynn preceded Casey, as did also Jimmy Blake,
and the former was a lulu and the latter was a fake,
so upon that stricken multitude grim melancholy sat,
for there seemed but little chance of Casey's getting to the bat.

But Flynn let drive a single, to the wonderment of all,
and Blake, the much despised, tore the cover off the ball;
and when the dust had lifted, and the men saw what had occurred,
there was Jimmy safe at second and Flynn a-hugging third.

Then from five thousand throats and more there rose a lusty yell;
it rumbled through the valley, it rattled in the dell;
it knocked upon the mountain and recoiled upon the flat,
for Casey, mighty Casey, was advancing to the bat.

There was ease in Casey's manner as he stepped into his place;
there was pride in Casey's bearing and a smile on Casey's face.
And when, responding to the cheers, he lightly doffed his hat,
no stranger in the crowd could doubt 'twas Casey at the bat.

Ten thousand eyes were on him as he rubbed his hands with dirt;
five thousand tongues applauded when he wiped them on his shirt.
Then while the writhing pitcher ground the ball into his hip,
defiance gleamed in Casey's eye, a sneer curled Casey's lip.

And now the leather-covered sphere came hurtling through the air,
and Casey stood a-watching it in haughty grandeur there.
Close by the sturdy batsman the ball unheeded sped--
"That ain't my style," said Casey. "Strike one," the umpire said.

From the benches, black with people, there went up a muffled roar,
like the beating of the storm-waves on a stern and distant shore.
"Kill him! Kill the umpire!" shouted someone on the stand;
and it's likely they'd have killed him had not Casey raised his hand.

With a smile of Christian charity great Casey's visage shone;
he stilled the rising tumult; he bade the game go on;
he signaled to the pitcher, and once more the spheroid flew;
but Casey still ignored it, and the umpire said: "Strike two."

"Fraud!" cried the maddened thousands, and echo answered fraud;
but one scornful look from Casey and the audience was awed.
They saw his face grow stern and cold, they saw his muscles strain,
and they knew that Casey wouldn't let that ball go by again.

The sneer is gone from Casey's lip, his teeth are clenched in hate;
he pounds with cruel violence his bat upon the plate.
And now the pitcher holds the ball, and now he lets it go,
and now the air is shattered by the force of Casey's blow.

Oh, somewhere in this favored land the sun is shining bright;
the band is playing somewhere, and somewhere hearts are light,
and somewhere men are laughing, and somewhere children shout;
but there is no joy in Mudville — mighty Casey has struck out.

Analyze the Poem:

This poem is about a baseball game. It is so famous that many people have actually memorized the poem and recite it with dramatic flair as if the game was actually happening. Describe 5 main ideas or things you understand from this poem about baseball.

1 _____

_____

2 _____

_____

3 _____

_____

4 _____

_____

5 _____

_____

Most stories have a happy ending but here Casey fails. It may be this unexpected surprise that makes this poem so memorable. Everyone knows what it is like to win and to lose. Describe a time when you were disappointed or lost unexpectedly. How did it feel? (It does not have to be about sports)

_____

_____

_____

_____

_____

_____

On the next page create a drawing to help illustrate this poem. You may think of it as a whole or choose to focus on one part. Include some of the text in a creative way.

Extended Exploration:

Write a short synopsis of the poem. What main idea or story was told?

_____

_____

_____

_____

_____

American writer Ernest Lawrence Thayer was born August 14, 1863 and died on August 21, 1940. He graduated with high honors in philosophy from Harvard University in 1885, where he had been editor of the Harvard Lampoon and a member of the theatrical society Hasty Pudding. During the mid-1890s, Thayer contributed several comic poems for Hearst's newspaper *New York Journal* and then began overseeing his family's mills in Worcester full-time.

Discover or research 5 more facts about the author or poem.

1 _____

_____

2 _____

_____

3 _____

_____

4 _____

_____

5 _____

_____

"The Raven" by Edgar Allan Poe

Once upon a midnight dreary, while I pondered, weak and weary,
Over many a quaint and curious volume of forgotten lore,
While I nodded, nearly napping, suddenly there came a tapping,
As of some one gently rapping, rapping at my chamber door.
"'Tis some visitor," I muttered, "tapping at my chamber door-
　　　　Only this, and nothing more."

Ah, distinctly I remember it was in the bleak December,
And each separate dying ember wrought its ghost upon the floor.
Eagerly I wished the morrow;- vainly I had sought to borrow
From my books surcease of sorrow- sorrow for the lost Lenore-
For the rare and radiant maiden whom the angels name Lenore-
　　　　Nameless *here* for evermore.

And the silken, sad, uncertain rustling of each purple curtain
Thrilled me- filled me with fantastic terrors never felt before;
So that now, to still the beating of my heart, I stood repeating,
"'Tis some visitor entreating entrance at my chamber door-
Some late visitor entreating entrance at my chamber door;-
　　　　This it is, and nothing more."

Presently my soul grew stronger; hesitating then no longer,
"Sir," said I, "or Madam, truly your forgiveness I implore;
But the fact is I was napping, and so gently you came rapping,
And so faintly you came tapping, tapping at my chamber door,
That I scarce was sure I heard you"- here I opened wide the door;-
　　　　Darkness there, and nothing more.

Deep into that darkness peering, long I stood there wondering, fearing,
Doubting, dreaming dreams no mortal ever dared to dream before;
But the silence was unbroken, and the stillness gave no token,
And the only word there spoken was the whispered word, "Lenore?"
This I whispered, and an echo murmured back the word, "Lenore!" -
　　　　Merely this, and nothing more.

Back into the chamber turning, all my soul within me burning,
Soon again I heard a tapping somewhat louder than before.
"Surely," said I, "surely that is something at my window lattice:
Let me see, then, what thereat is, and this mystery explore-
Let my heart be still a moment and this mystery explore;-
　　　　'Tis the wind and nothing more!"

Open here I flung the shutter, when, with many a flirt and flutter,
In there stepped a stately Raven of the saintly days of yore;
Not the least obeisance made he; not a minute stopped or stayed he;
But, with mien of lord or lady, perched above my chamber door-
Perched upon a bust of Pallas just above my chamber door-
　　　　Perched, and sat, and nothing more.

Then this ebony bird beguiling my sad fancy into smiling,
By the grave and stern decorum of the countenance it wore,
"Though thy crest be shorn and shaven, thou," I said, "art sure no craven,
Ghastly grim and ancient Raven wandering from the Nightly shore-
Tell me what thy lordly name is on the Night's Plutonian shore!"
　　　　Quoth the Raven, "Nevermore."

Much I marvelled this ungainly fowl to hear discourse so plainly,
Though its answer little meaning- little relevancy bore;
For we cannot help agreeing that no living human being
Ever yet was blessed with seeing bird above his chamber door-
Bird or beast upon the sculptured bust above his chamber door,
　　　　With such name as "Nevermore."

But the Raven, sitting lonely on the placid bust, spoke only
That one word, as if his soul in that one word he did outpour.
Nothing further then he uttered- not a feather then he fluttered-
Till I scarcely more than muttered, "Other friends have flown before-
On the morrow *he* will leave me, as my hopes have flown before."
　　　　Then the bird said, "Nevermore."

Startled at the stillness broken by reply so aptly spoken,
"Doubtless," said I, "what it utters is its only stock and store,
Caught from some unhappy master whom unmerciful Disaster
Followed fast and followed faster till his songs one burden bore-
Till the dirges of his Hope that melancholy burden bore
　　　　Of 'Never- nevermore.'"

But the Raven still beguiling all my fancy into smiling,
Straight I wheeled a cushioned seat in front of bird, and bust and door;
Then upon the velvet sinking, I betook myself to linking
Fancy unto fancy, thinking what this ominous bird of yore-
What this grim, ungainly, ghastly, gaunt and ominous bird of yore
　　　　Meant in croaking "Nevermore."

This I sat engaged in guessing, but no syllable expressing
To the fowl whose fiery eyes now burned into my bosom's core;
This and more I sat divining, with my head at ease reclining
On the cushion's velvet lining that the lamp-light gloated o'er,
But whose velvet violet lining with the lamp-light gloating o'er,
　　　　She shall press, ah, nevermore!

Then methought the air grew denser, perfumed from an unseen censer
Swung by Seraphim whose footfalls tinkled on the tufted floor.
"Wretch," I cried, "thy God hath lent thee- by these angels he hath sent thee
Respite- respite and nepenthe, from thy memories of Lenore!
Quaff, oh quaff this kind nepenthe and forget this lost Lenore!"
　　　　Quoth the Raven, "Nevermore."

"Prophet!" said I, "thing of evil!- prophet still, if bird or devil!-
Whether Tempter sent, or whether tempest tossed thee here ashore,
Desolate yet all undaunted, on this desert land enchanted-
On this home by Horror haunted- tell me truly, I implore-
Is there- *is* there balm in Gilead?- tell me- tell me, I implore!"
　　　　Quoth the Raven, "Nevermore."

"Prophet!" said I, "thing of evil! - prophet still, if bird or devil!
By that Heaven that bends above us- by that God we both adore-
Tell this soul with sorrow laden if, within the distant Aidenn,
It shall clasp a sainted maiden whom the angels name Lenore-
Clasp a rare and radiant maiden whom the angels name Lenore."
　　　　Quoth the Raven, "Nevermore."

"Be that word our sign in parting, bird or fiend," I shrieked, upstarting-
"Get thee back into the tempest and the Night's Plutonian shore!
Leave no black plume as a token of that lie thy soul hath spoken!
Leave my loneliness unbroken!- quit the bust above my door!
Take thy beak from out my heart, and take thy form from off my door!"
　　　　Quoth the Raven, "Nevermore."

And the Raven, never flitting, still is sitting, *still* is sitting
On the pallid bust of Pallas just above my chamber door;
And his eyes have all the seeming of a demon's that is dreaming,
And the lamp-light o'er him streaming throws his shadow on the floor;
And my soul from out that shadow that lies floating on the floor
　　　　Shall be lifted- nevermore!

Analyze the Poem:

This poem is rather dark and scary. It is so famous that many people have actually memorized the poem and recite it around Halloween. Write 5 main ideas or things you understand from this scary poem.

1 _____

_____

2 _____

_____

3 _____

_____

4 _____

_____

5 _____

_____

What is it about this poem that makes it scary? Include examples from the poem in your answer.

_____

_____

_____

_____

_____

On the next page create a drawing to help illustrate this poem. You may think of it as a whole or choose to focus on one part. Include some of the text in a creative way.

Extended Exploration:

Write a short synopsis of the poem. What main idea or story was told?

_____
_____
_____
_____
_____

Edgar Allan Poe was born January 19, 1809 and died October 7, 1849. An American writer, editor, and literary critic, Poe is best known for his poetry and short stories, particularly his tales of mystery and the macabre. He is widely regarded as a central figure of Romanticism in the United States and American literature as a whole, and he was one of the country's earliest writers of the short story format. Poe is generally considered the inventor of detective fiction and is credited with contributing to the emerging genre of science fiction. He was the first well-known American writer who tried to earn a living through writing alone which resulted in a financially difficult life and career.

Discover or research 5 more facts about the author or poem.

1 _____
_____

2 _____
_____

3 _____
_____

4 _____
_____

5 _____
_____

"Life" by Charlotte Brontë

Life, believe, is not a dream
So dark as sages say;
Oft a little morning rain
Foretells a pleasant day.
Sometimes there are clouds of gloom,
But these are transient all;
If the shower will make the roses bloom,
O why lament its fall?

Rapidly, merrily,
Life's sunny hours flit by,
Gratefully, cheerily
Enjoy them as they fly!

What though Death at times steps in,
And calls our Best away?
What though sorrow seems to win,
O'er hope, a heavy sway?
Yet hope again elastic springs,
Unconquered, though she fell;
Still buoyant are her golden wings,
Still strong to bear us well.

Manfully, fearlessly,
The day of trial bear,
For gloriously, victoriously,
Can courage quell despair!

Analyze the Poem:

This short poem has four stanzas. Write the main idea from each below.

1 _____

_____

2 _____

_____

3 _____

_____

4 _____

_____

An allegory is a story, poem, or picture that can be interpreted to reveal a hidden meaning, usually a moral or political one. What might be the main message of this poem? Include an example from the poem to make your point.

_____
_____
_____
_____
_____
_____
_____

On the next page create a drawing around the text of the poem to help illustrate the meaning.

"Life" by Charlotte Brontë

Life, believe, is not a dream
So dark as sages say;
Oft a little morning rain
Foretells a pleasant day.
Sometimes there are clouds of gloom,
But these are transient all;
If the shower will make the roses bloom,
O why lament its fall?

Rapidly, merrily,
Life's sunny hours flit by,
Gratefully, cheerily
Enjoy them as they fly!

What though Death at times steps in,
And calls our Best away?
What though sorrow seems to win,
O'er hope, a heavy sway?
Yet hope again elastic springs,
Unconquered, though she fell;
Still buoyant are her golden wings,
Still strong to bear us well.

Manfully, fearlessly,
The day of trial bear,
For gloriously, victoriously,
Can courage quell despair!

Extended Exploration:

Write a short synopsis of the poem. What main idea or story was told?

_____

_____

_____

_____

_____

Charlotte Brontë was born on April 21, 1816 and died March 31, 1855. An English novelist and poet, she was the eldest of the three Brontë sisters who survived into adulthood and whose novels have become classics of English literature. She first published her works–including her best known novel, *Jane Eyre*– under the pen name Currer Bell. She was persuaded by her publisher to make occasional visits to London, where she revealed her true identity and began to move in more famous social circles.

Discover or research 5 more facts about the author or poem.

1 _____

_____

2 _____

_____

3 _____

_____

4 _____

_____

5 _____

_____

"Sonnet XLIII" by Elizabeth Barrett Browning

How do I love thee? Let me count the ways.
I love thee to the depth and breadth and height
My soul can reach, when feeling out of sight
For the ends of Being and ideal Grace.
I love thee to the level of everyday's
Most quiet need, by sun and candlelight.
I love thee freely, as men strive for Right;
I love thee purely, as they turn from Praise.
I love thee with the passion put to use
In my old griefs, and with my childhood's faith.
I love thee with a love I seemed to lose
With my lost saints, I love thee with the breath,
Smiles, tears, of all my life! and, if God choose,
I shall but love thee better after death.

Analyze the Poem:

This poem describes love, literally counting the many ways the author loves her subject. List five ways that Elizabeth describes the depth of her love.

1 _____

_____

2 _____

_____

3 _____

_____

4 _____

_____

5 _____

_____

Considering the idea of love, write 3 different ways you could describe love. Do it in a poetic way.

1 _____

_____

2 _____

_____

3 _____

_____

Create a drawing on the next page based on the idea of love. Draw it around the poem.

"Sonnet XLIII"
by Elizabeth Barrett Browning

How do I love thee? Let me count the ways.
I love thee to the depth and breadth and height
My soul can reach, when feeling out of sight
For the ends of Being and ideal Grace.
I love thee to the level of everyday's
Most quiet need, by sun and candlelight.
I love thee freely, as men strive for Right;
I love thee purely, as they turn from Praise.
I love thee with the passion put to use
In my old griefs, and with my childhood's faith.
I love thee with a love I seemed to lose
With my lost saints, I love thee with the breath,
Smiles, tears, of all my life! and, if God choose,
I shall but love thee better after death.

Extended Exploration:

Write a short synopsis of the poem. What main idea or story was told?

_____

_____

_____

_____

_____

Elizabeth Barrett Browning was born March 6, 1806 and died June 29, 1861. She was one of the most prominent English poets of the Victorian era, popular in both Britain and the United States during her lifetime. The eldest of 12 children, she wrote poetry from about the age of six. Her mother's collection of Elizabeth's poems forms one of the largest surviving collections of writings produced in one's youth by any English writer. Elizabeth campaigned for the abolition of slavery and her work helped influence reform in the child labor legislation. Elizabeth's work had a major influence on prominent writers of the day, including Edgar Allan Poe and Emily Dickinson.

Discover or research 5 more facts about the author or poem.

1 _____

_____

2 _____

_____

3 _____

_____

4 _____

_____

5 _____

_____

"We Wear The Mask" by Paul Laurence Dunbar

We wear the mask that grins and lies,
It hides our cheeks and shades our eyes,--
This debt we pay to human guile;
With torn and bleeding hearts we smile,
And mouth with myriad subtleties.

Why should the world be over-wise,
In counting all our tears and sighs?
Nay, let them only see us, while
We wear the mask.

We smile, but, O great Christ, our cries
To thee from tortured souls arise.
We sing, but oh the clay is vile
Beneath our feet, and long the mile;
But let the world dream otherwise,
We wear the mask!

Analyze the Poem:

The poem recognizes suffering and the need to hide pain to live on. Write below what you understand from each stanza.

1 _____

2 _____

3 _____

Illustrations help tell a story. What three things can you draw to help illustrate this poem?

1 _____

2 _____

3 _____

On the next page create a drawing to help illustrate this poem. Use one or more of the ideas you described above. Include some of the text in a creative way.

Extended Exploration:

Write a short synopsis of the poem. What main idea or story was told?

_____

_____

_____

_____

_____

Paul Laurence Dunbar was born June 27, 1872 and died February 9, 1906. He was an American poet, novelist, and playwright of the late 19th and early 20th centuries. Paul was born in Dayton, Ohio, to parents who had been enslaved in Kentucky before the American Civil War. Dunbar began to write stories and poems when still a child. He was president of his high school's literary society. He published his first poems at the age of 16 in a Dayton newspaper.

Discover or research 5 more facts about the author or poem.

1 _____

2 _____

3 _____

4 _____

5 _____

"On The Bridge" by Kate Greenaway

If I could see a little fish
That is what I just now wish!
I want to see his great round eyes
Always open in surprise.

I wish a water rat would glide
Slowly to the other side;
Or a dancing spider sit
On the yellow flags a bit.

I think I'll get some stones to throw,
And watch the pretty circles show.
Or shall we sail a flower-boat,
And watch it slowly, slowly float?

That's nice because you never know
How far away it means to go;
And when to-morrow comes, you see,
It may be in the great wide sea.

Analyze the Poem:

This short poem has four stanzas. Write the main idea from each below.

1 _____

2 _____

3 _____

4 _____

In the second stanza the author makes a wish that includes a rat and spider. Try changing that four line stanza to your own wish. The first two lines should rhyme; so should the second two.

I wish..._____

_____

_____

Do you like Greenaway's version or your idea better? Why?

_____

_____

On the next page create a drawing around the text of the poem to help illustrate the meaning.

"On The Bridge"
by Kate Greenaway

If I could see a little fish
That is what I just now wish!
I want to see his great round eyes
Always open in surprise.

I wish a water rat would glide
Slowly to the other side;
Or a dancing spider sit
On the yellow flags a bit.

I think I'll get some stones to throw,
And watch the pretty circles show.
Or shall we sail a flower-boat,
And watch it slowly, slowly float?

That's nice because you never know
How far away it means to go;
And when to-morrow comes, you see,
It may be in the great wide sea.

Extended Exploration:

Write a short synopsis of the poem. What main idea or story was told?

_____

_____

_____

_____

_____

Catherine "Kate" Greenaway, born March 17, 1846 and died on November 6, 1901. She was an English children's book illustrator and writer. Greenaway spent much of her childhood at Rolleston, Nottinghamshire. She studied at what is now the Royal College of Art in London. Her first book, *Under the Window* (1879), was a best-seller. It was a collection of simple, perfectly idyllic verses about children.

Discover or research 5 more facts about the author or poem.

1 _____

2 _____

3 _____

4 _____

5 _____

"Trees" by Alfred Joyce Kilmer

I think that I shall never see
A poem lovely as a tree.

A tree whose hungry mouth is prest
Against the earth's sweet flowing breast;

A tree that looks at God all day,
And lifts her leafy arms to pray;

A tree that may in Summer wear
A nest of robins in her hair;

Upon whose bosom snow has lain;
Who intimately lives with rain.

Poems are made by fools like me,
But only God can make a tree.

Analyze the Poem:

This short poem is about a tree and uses four creative ways to describe it. We have described the first one, you describe the other three.

1 The tree is like a baby drinking mother's milk, but from the earth. _____

2 _____

_____

3 _____

_____

4 _____

_____

What are 4 more comparisons or symbolic ideas you could make using a tree?

1 _____

_____

2 _____

_____

3 _____

_____

4 _____

_____

On the next page create a drawing around the text of the poem to help illustrate the meaning.

"Trees"
by Alfred Joyce Kilmer

I think that I shall never see
A poem lovely as a tree.

A tree whose hungry mouth is prest
Against the earth's sweet flowing breast;

A tree that looks at God all day,
And lifts her leafy arms to pray;

A tree that may in Summer wear
A nest of robins in her hair;

Upon whose bosom snow has lain;
Who intimately lives with rain.

Poems are made by fools like me,
But only God can make a tree.

Extended Exploration:

Write a short synopsis of the poem. What main idea or story was told?

_____

_____

_____

_____

_____

Joyce Kilmer was born December 6, 1886 and died July 30, 1918. He was an American writer and prolific poet whose works celebrated the common beauty of the natural world as well as his religious faith. Kilmer was also a journalist, literary critic, lecturer, and editor. Though he was a popular poet, his peers did not take his work seriously. Many writers have parodied Kilmer's work and style, as attested by the many parodies of this poem, "Trees."

Discover or research 5 more facts about the author or poem.

1 _____

_____

2 _____

_____

3 _____

_____

4 _____

_____

5 _____

_____

"Roofs" by Alfred Joyce Kilmer

The road is wide and the stars are out and the breath of the night is sweet,
And this is the time when wanderlust should seize upon my feet.
But I'm glad to turn from the open road and the starlight on my face,
And to leave the splendor of out-of-doors for a human dwelling place.

I never have seen a vagabond who really liked to roam
All up and down the streets of the world and not to have a home:
The tramp who slept in your barn last night and left at break of day
Will wander only until he finds another place to stay.

A gypsy-man will sleep in his cart with canvas overhead;
Or else he'll go into his tent when it is time for bed.
He'll sit on the grass and take his ease so long as the sun is high,
But when it is dark he wants a roof to keep away the sky.

If you call a gypsy a vagabond, I think you do him wrong,
For he never goes a-travelling but he takes his home along.
And the only reason a road is good, as every wanderer knows,
Is just because of the homes, the homes, the homes to which it goes.

They say that life is a highway and its milestones are the years,
And now and then there's a toll-gate where you buy your way with tears.
It's a rough road and a steep road and it stretches broad and far,
But at last it leads to a golden Town where golden Houses are.

Analyze the Poem:

This short poem has five stanzas. Write the main idea or what you understand from each below.

1 _____

_____

2 _____

_____

3 _____

_____

4 _____

_____

5 _____

_____

This poem begins with the idea that traveling is a fun adventure but ends with the thoughts that life can be difficult, home is where we all want to be and where we feel safe. Describe a time you had fun away from home but also felt homesick and wanted to return.

_____

_____

_____

_____

_____

Create a drawing on the next page based on a stanza your teacher assigned or your favorite one.

Extended Exploration:

Write a short synopsis of the poem. What main idea or story was told?

_____

_____

_____

_____

_____

Joyce Kilmer was born December 6, 1886 and died July 30, 1918. He was an American writer and prolific poet whose works celebrated the common beauty of the natural world as well as his religious faith. Kilmer was also a journalist, literary critic, lecturer, and editor. Though he was a popular poet, his peers did not take his work seriously. Many writers have parodied Kilmer's work and style, as attested by the many parodies of "Trees."

Discover or research 5 more facts about the author or poem.

1 _____

_____

2 _____

_____

3 _____

_____

4 _____

_____

5 _____

_____

"City Trees" by Edna St. Vincent Millay

The trees along this city street,
Save for the traffic and the trains,
Would make a sound as thin and sweet
As trees in country lanes.

And people standing in their shade
Out of a shower, undoubtedly
Would hear such music as is made
Upon a country tree.

Oh, little leaves that are so dumb *(silent)*
Against the shrieking city air,
I watch you when the wind has come,—
I know what sound is there.

Analyze the Poem:

This short poem has three stanzas. Write the main idea from each below.

1 _____

_____

2 _____

_____

Note: The word *dumb* means silent, because they cannot speak. It does not mean stupid.

3 _____

_____

Edna Millay's poem tries to point out something most people ignore—the little trees of the city. There are many things we ignore because we are too busy. What is something you or your friends ignore but would miss if it was gone?

_____

Write a short four line stanza about the thing written above. Write the way Edna Millay did by rhyming the first and third lines and rhyming the second and last line of the stanza.

_____

_____

_____

_____

On the next page create a drawing around the text of the poem to help illustrate the meaning. If you include a street, try to make it look 3-D if you can, using the rules of perspective.

"City Trees"
by Edna St. Vincent Millay

The trees along this city street,
Save for the traffic and the trains,
Would make a sound as thin and sweet
As trees in country lanes.

And people standing in their shade
Out of a shower, undoubtedly
Would hear such music as is made
Upon a country tree.

Oh, little leaves that are so dumb (silent)
Against the shrieking city air,
I watch you when the wind has come,—
I know what sound is there.

Extended Exploration:

Write a short synopsis of the poem. What main idea or story was told?

_____

_____

_____

_____

_____

Edna St. Vincent Millay was born February 22, 1892 and died October 19, 1950. She was an American poet and playwright known for her feminist activism. She received the Pulitzer Prize for Poetry in 1923, the third woman to win the award for poetry. Edna used the pseudonym Nancy Boyd for her prose work. The poet Richard Wilbur asserted, "She wrote some of the best sonnets of the century."

Discover or research 5 more facts about the author or poem.

1 _____

_____

2 _____

_____

3 _____

_____

4 _____

_____

5 _____

_____

"As Long As Your Eyes Are Blue" by Banjo Paterson

"Will you love me, sweet, when my hair is grey
And my cheeks shall have lost their hue?
When the charms of youth shall have passed away
Will your love as of old prove true?

"For the looks may change, and the heart may range
And the love be no longer fond;
Will you love with truth in the years of youth
And away to the years beyond?"

Oh, I love you, sweet, for your locks of brown
And the blush on your cheek that lies,
But I love you most for the kindly heart
That I see in your sweet blue eyes.

For the eyes are the signs of the soul within,
Of the heart that is leal and true,
And, my own sweetheart, I shall love you still,
Just as long as your eyes are blue.

For the locks may bleach, and the cheeks of peach
May be reft of their golden hue;
But, my own sweetheart, I shall love you still,
Just as long as your eyes are blue.

Analyze the Poem:

This short poem has five stanzas. Write the main idea or what you understand from each below.

1 _____

_____

2 _____

_____

3 _____

_____

4 _____

_____

5 _____

_____

An allegory is a story, poem, or picture that can be interpreted to reveal a hidden meaning. This poem is about love and aging. What is the poet's message to the reader?

_____

_____

_____

_____

_____

On the next page create a drawing around the text of the poem to help illustrate the meaning.

"As Long As Your Eyes Are Blue"
by Banjo Paterson

"Will you love me, sweet, when my hair is grey
And my cheeks shall have lost their hue?
When the charms of youth shall have passed away
Will your love as of old prove true?

"For the looks may change, and the heart may range
And the love be no longer fond;
Will you love with truth in the years of youth
And away to the years beyond?"

Oh, I love you, sweet, for your locks of brown
And the blush on your cheek that lies,
But I love you most for the kindly heart
That I see in your sweet blue eyes.

For the eyes are the signs of the soul within,
Of the heart that is leal and true,
And, my own sweetheart, I shall love you still,
Just as long as your eyes are blue.

For the locks may bleach, and the cheeks of peach
May be reft of their golden hue;
But, my own sweetheart, I shall love you still,
Just as long as your eyes are blue.

Extended Exploration:

Write a short synopsis of the poem. What main idea or story was told?

_____

_____

_____

_____

_____

Andrew Barton "Banjo" Paterson, born February 17, 1864 and died February 5, 1941. He was an Australian bush poet, journalist and author who wrote many ballads and poems about Australian life. He focused particularly on the rural and outback areas where he spent much of his childhood. Paterson's more notable poems include "Waltzing Matilda," "The Man from Snowy River," and "Clancy of the Overflow."

Discover or research 5 more facts about the author or poem.

1 _____

_____

2 _____

_____

3 _____

_____

4 _____

_____

5 _____

_____

"Song" by Christina Georgina Rossetti

Two doves upon the selfsame branch,
Two lilies on a single stem,
Two butterflies upon one flower:--
Oh happy they who look on them.

Who look upon them hand in hand
Flushed in the rosy summer light;
Who look upon them hand in hand
And never give a thought to night.

Analyze the Poem:

This short poem has just two stanzas. Write the main idea or what you understand from each below.

1 _____

_____

_____

2 _____

_____

_____

Though this poem speaks about doves, lilies, and butterflies, the real focus is on the people looking at these things. This is an allegory: a story, poem, or picture that can be interpreted to reveal a hidden meaning, usually a moral or political one. What is the message of this poem?

_____

_____

_____

_____

_____

_____

_____

On the next page create a drawing or decorative border for the poem around the text to help illustrate the meaning.

"Song"
by Christina Georgina Rossetti

Two doves upon the selfsame branch,
Two lilies on a single stem,
Two butterflies upon one flower:--
Oh happy they who look on them.

Who look upon them hand in hand
Flushed in the rosy summer light;
Who look upon them hand in hand
And never give a thought to night.

Extended Exploration:

Write a short synopsis of the poem. What main idea or story was told?

_____

_____

_____

_____

_____

Christina Georgina Rossetti born December 5, 1830 and died December 29, 1894. She was an English poet who wrote a variety of romantic, religious, and children's poems. She is famous for writing *Goblin Market* and *Remember*, and the words of the Christmas carol *In the Bleak Midwinter*. Rossetti started writing poems at the age of 12; by 17 she began experimenting with verse forms such as sonnets, hymns, and ballads. She sometimes used the pen-name "Ellen Alleyne."

Discover or research 5 more facts about the author or poem.

1 _____

_____

2 _____

_____

3 _____

_____

4 _____

_____

5 _____

_____

"Miniver Cheevy" by Edwin Arlington Robinson

Miniver Cheevy, child of scorn,
Grew lean while he assailed the seasons;
He wept that he was ever born,
And he had reasons.

Miniver loved the days of old
When swords were bright and steeds were prancing;
The vision of a warrior bold
Would set him dancing.

Miniver sighed for what was not,
And dreamed and rested from his labors;
He dreamed of Thebes and Camelot
And Priam's neighbors.

Miniver mourned the ripe renown
That made so many a name so fragrant;
He mourned Romance, now on the town,
And Art, a vagrant.

Miniver loved the Medici,
Albeit he had never seen one;
He would have sinned incessantly
Could he have been one.

Miniver cursed the commonplace,
And eyed a khaki suit with loathing;
He missed the mediaeval grace
Of iron clothing.

Miniver scorned the gold he sought,
But sore annoyed he was without it;
Miniver thought and thought and thought
And thought about it.

Miniver Cheevy, born too late,
Scratched his head and kept on thinking;
Miniver coughed, and called it fate,
And kept on drinking.

Analyze the Poem:

This poem is about a character named Miniver Cheevy who misses "the good old days." You may have heard people say "back in my day..." or "When I was a kid..." and tell you how things were better back then. List five things Miniver Cheevy wishes for or misses.

1 _____

_____

2 _____

_____

3 _____

_____

4 _____

_____

5 _____

_____

Things change as we get older. Today, almost everyone has a computer in their home, but that was not true until recently. With computers there are new problems of privacy; everything you do online can be tracked and traced. What is something you miss from when you were younger? Why do you miss it?

_____

_____

_____

_____

_____

On the next page create a drawing to help illustrate this poem. You may think of it as a whole or choose to focus on one part. Include some of the text in a creative way.

Extended Exploration:

Write a short synopsis of the poem. What main idea or story was told?

_____

_____

_____

_____

_____

_____

Edwin Arlington Robinson was born December 22, 1869 and died April 6, 1935. He was an American poet who was awarded three Pulitzer Prizes for his work. His father died while he was young and Edwin became the man of the household. He tried farming but later moved to New York where he led a difficult life as a poor poet while making friendships with other writers, artists, and would-be intellectuals. In 1896 he self-published his first book, *The Torrent and the Night Before*, paying 100 dollars for 500 copies.

Discover or research 5 more facts about the author or poem.

1 _____

_____

2 _____

_____

3 _____

_____

4 _____

_____

5 _____

_____

"The Knight's Song" by Lewis Carroll

I'll tell thee everything I can:
There's little to relate.
I saw an aged aged man,
A-sitting on a gate.

'Who are you, aged man?' I said.
'And how is it you live?'
And his answer trickled through my head,
Like water through a sieve.
He said, 'I look for butterflies
That sleep among the wheat:
I make them into mutton-pies,
And sell them in the street.

I sell them unto men,' he said,
'Who sail on stormy seas;
And that's the way I get my bread,
A trifle, if you please.'
But I was thinking of a plan
To dye one's whiskers green,
And always use so large a fan
That they could not be seen.

So having no reply to give
To what the old man said, I cried
'Come, tell me how you live!'
And thumped him on the head.
His accents mild took up the tale:

He said 'I go my ways,
And when I find a mountain-rill,
I set it in a blaze;
And thence they make a stuff they call
Rowland's Macassar-Oil,
Yet two pence-halfpenny is all
They give me for my toil.'

But I was thinking of a way
To feed oneself on batter,
And so go on from day to day '
Getting a little fatter.
I shook him well from side to side,
Until his face was blue:
'Come, tell me how you live,' I cried,
'And what it is you do!'

He said, 'I hunt for haddocks' eyes
Among the heather bright,
And work them into waistcoat-buttons
In the silent night.
And these I do not sell for gold
Or coin of silvery shine,
But for a copper halfpenny,
And that will purchase nine.

'I sometimes dig for buttered rolls,
Or set limed twigs for crabs:
I sometimes search the grassy knolls
For wheels of Hansom-cabs.
And that's the way' (he gave a wink)
'By which I get my wealth,
And very gladly will I drink
Your Honor's noble health.'

I heard him then, for I had just
Completed my design
To keep the Menai bridge from rust
By boiling it in wine.
I thanked him much for telling me
The way he got his wealth,
But chiefly for his wish that he
Might drink my noble health.

And now, if e'er by chance I put
My fingers into glue,
Or madly squeeze a right-hand foot
Into a left-hand shoe,
Or if I drop upon my toe
A very heavy weight,
I weep, for it reminds me so
Of that old man I used to know,

Whose look was mild, whose speech was slow
Whose hair was whiter than the snow,
Whose face was very like a crow,
With eyes, like cinders, all aglow,
Who seemed distracted with his woe,
Who rocked his body to and fro,
And muttered mumblingly and low,
As if his mouth were full of dough,
Who snorted like a buffalo-
That summer evening long ago,
A-sitting on a gate.

Analyze the Poem:

This is one of Lewis Carroll's nonsense poems. Much of it is rather silly, or simply does not make sense. Find five things from this poem you feel are strange or odd and write them below.

1 _____

_____

2 _____

_____

3 _____

_____

4 _____

_____

5 _____

_____

Though the poem is odd, what do you think is the old man's problem? What makes him so odd? Include something from the poem to prove your point of view.

_____

_____

_____

_____

_____

_____

On the next page create a drawing to help illustrate this poem. You may think of it as a whole or choose to focus on one part. Include some of the text in a creative way.

Extended Exploration:

Write a short synopsis of the poem. What main idea or story was told?

_____

_____

_____

_____

_____

Lewis Carroll was born Charles Lutwidge Dodgson on January 27, 1832 and died January 14, 1898. He was an English writer, mathematician, logician, Anglican deacon, and photographer. His most famous writings are *Alice's Adventures in Wonderland* and its sequel *Through the Looking-Glass*. The latter includes the poem *Jabberwocky* and is an example of the genre of literary nonsense. Carroll is noted for his facility at word play, logic and fantasy.

Discover or research 5 more facts about the author or poem.

1 _____

_____

2 _____

_____

3 _____

_____

4 _____

_____

5 _____

_____

"Lady Icicle" by Emily Pauline Johnson

Little Lady Icicle is dreaming in the north-land
And gleaming in the north-land, her pillow all a-glow;
For the frost has come and found her
With an ermine robe around her
Where little Lady Icicle lies dreaming in the snow.

Little Lady Icicle is waking in the north-land,
And shaking in the north-land her pillow to and fro;
And the hurricane a-skirling
Sends the feathers all a-whirling
Where little Lady Icicle is waking in the snow.

Little Lady Icicle is laughing in the north-land,
And quaffing in the north-land her wines that overflow;
All the lakes and rivers crusting
That her finger-tips are dusting,
Where little Lady Icicle is laughing in the snow.

Little Lady Icicle is singing in the north-land,
And bringing from the north-land a music wild and low;
And the fairies watch and listen
Where her silver slippers glisten,
As little Lady Icicle goes singing through the snow.

Little Lady Icicle is coming from the north-land,
Benumbing all the north-land where'er her feet may go;
With a fringe of frost before her
And a crystal garment o'er her,
Little Lady Icicle is coming with the snow.

Analyze the Poem:

This short poem has five stanzas about Lady Icicle. Write the main idea or what you understand from each stanza below.

1 _____

_____

2 _____

_____

3 _____

_____

4 _____

_____

5 _____

_____

An allegory is a story, poem, or picture that can be interpreted to reveal a hidden meaning. What do you think Lady Icicle symbolizes? Include information from the poem in your answer.

_____

_____

_____

_____

_____

_____

On the next page create a drawing to help illustrate this poem. You may think of it as a whole or choose to focus on one part. Include some of the text in a creative way.

Extended Exploration:

Write a short synopsis of the poem. What main idea or story was told?

_____

_____

_____

_____

_____

Emily Pauline Johnson was born at Chiefswood on March 10, 1861 and died March 7, 1913. Known as E. Pauline Johnson or just Pauline Johnson, she was a Canadian writer and performer popular in the late 19th century. Johnson was notable for her poems and performances that celebrated her Aboriginal heritage; her father was a hereditary Mohawk chief of mixed ancestry. She also drew from English influences, as her mother was an English immigrant. She was known in Mohawk as Tekahionwake which is pronounced dageh-eeon-wageh and means 'double-life.'

Discover or research 5 more facts about the author or poem.

1 _____

_____

2 _____

_____

3 _____

_____

4 _____

_____

5 _____

_____

"Jack And Jill" by Clara Doty Bates

Little boys, sit still--
Girls, too, if you will--
And let me tell you of Jack and Jill;
For I think another
Such sister and brother
Were never the children of one mother!

For an idle lad,
As he was, Jack had
No traits, after all, that were very bad.
He, was simply Jack,
With the coat on his back
Patched up in all colors from gray to black.

Both feet were bare;
And I do declare
That he never washed his face; and his hair
Was the color of straw--
You never saw
Such a crop--as long as the moral law!

When he went to school,
It was the rule
(Though 'twas hard to say he was really a fool)
To send him in at once,
So thick was his sconce,
To the block that was kept for the greatest dunce.

And Jill! no lass
Scarce ever has
Made bigger tracks on the country grass;
For her only fun
Was to romp and run,
Bare-headed, bare-footed, in wind and sun.

Wherever went Jack,
Close on his track,
With hair unbraided and down her back,
Loud-voiced and shrill,
She followed, until
No one said "Jack" without saying "Jill."

But to succeed
In teaching to read
Such a harum-scarum, was work indeed!
And I'm forced to tell
That her way to spell
Her name was with only a single 'l.'

Yet they were content.
One day they were sent
To the hill for water, and they went.
They did not drown,
But Jack fell down,
With a pail in his hand, and broke his crown!

And Jill, who must go
And always do
Exactly as Jack did, tumbled too!
Just think, if you will,
How they rolled down hill--
Straw-headed Jack and bare-footed Jill!

But up Jack got,
And home did trot,
Nor cared whether Jill was hurt or not;
While his poor bruised knob
Did burn and throb,
Tear falling on tear, sob following sob!

He could run the faster,
So a paper plaster
Had bound up the sight of his disaster
Before Jill came;
And the thoughtful dame,
For a break in her head, had fixed the same.

But Jill came in,
With a saucy grin
At seeing the plight poor Jack was in;
And when she saw
That bundle of straw
(His hair) bound up with a cloth, and his jaw

Tied up in white,
The comical sight
Made her clap her hands and laugh outright!
The dame, perplexed
And dreadfully vexed,
Got a stick and said, "I'll whip her next!"

How many blows fell
I will not tell,
But she did it in earnest, she did it well,
Till the naughty back
Was blue and black,
And Jill needed a plaster as much as Jack!

The next time, though,
Jack has to go
To the hill for water, I almost know
That bothering Jill
Will go up the hill,
And if he falls again, why, of course she will!

Analyze the Poem:

This poem is based on the old children's rhyme "Jack and Jill" from 1765. You may have learned it when you were young, but this version has many more details. List five interesting parts to this poetic story.

1 _____

2 _____

3 _____

4 _____

5 _____

This poem tells the story of two children, Jack and Jill. Based on the poem what can you say about each?

*Jack is...*_____

*Jill is...*_____

On the next page create a drawing to help illustrate this poem. You may think of it as a whole or choose to focus on one part. Include some of the text in a creative way.

Extended Exploration:

Write a short synopsis of the poem. What main idea or story was told?

_____

_____

_____

_____

_____

Clara Doty Bates was born on December 22, 1838 and died on October 14, 1895. She wrote many children's poems and fairy tales. Her family was descended from original pilgrims of the Mayflower and she was related to George Washington. She began writing at the young age of 10 and continued throughout her life.

Because information about her is hard to find, please find the titles of 5 more poems she wrote.

1 _____

_____

2 _____

_____

3 _____

_____

4 _____

_____

5 _____

_____

"Annabel Lee" by Edgar Allan Poe

It was many and many a year ago,
In a kingdom by the sea,
That a maiden there lived whom you may know
By the name of Annabel Lee;
And this maiden she lived with no other thought
Than to love and be loved by me.

I was a child and she was a child,
In this kingdom by the sea;
But we loved with a love that was more than love,
I and my Annabel Lee;
With a love that the winged seraphs of heaven
Coveted her and me.

And this was the reason that, long ago,
In this kingdom by the sea,
A wind blew out of a cloud, chilling
My beautiful Annabel Lee;
So that her highborn kinsman came
And bore her away from me,
To shut her up in a sepulchre *(tomb)*
In this kingdom by the sea.

The angels, not half so happy in heaven,
Went envying her and me,
Yes!, that was the reason (as all men know,
In this kingdom by the sea)
That the wind came out of the cloud by night,
Chilling and killing my Annabel Lee.

But our love it was stronger by far than the love
Of those who were older than we,
Of many far wiser than we,
And neither the angels in heaven above,
Nor the demons down under the sea,
Can ever dissever my soul from the soul
Of the beautiful Annabel Lee.

For the moon never beams without bringing me dreams
Of the beautiful Annabel Lee;
And the stars never rise but I feel the bright eyes
Of the beautiful Annabel Lee;
And so, all the night-tide, I lie down by the side
Of my darling, my darling, my life and my bride,
In the sepulchre there by the sea,
In her tomb by the sounding sea.

Analyze the Poem:

This poem has six stanzas. Write the main idea or what you understand from each below.

1 _____

_____

2 _____

_____

3 _____

_____

4 _____

_____

5 _____

_____

6 _____

_____

Edgar Allen Poe was known for writing sad and scary stories and poems. Some call him the Tim Burton of the 1800s. Imagine you were going to make a movie about this poem. What details would you put in the movie and explain how or why you would include them? Suggest the actors you would want to hire.

_____

_____

_____

_____

_____

On the next page create a drawing to help illustrate this poem. You may think of it as a whole or choose to focus on one part. Include some of the text in a creative way.

Extended Exploration:

Write a short synopsis of the poem. What main idea or story was told?

_____

_____

_____

_____

_____

Edgar Allan Poe was born January 19, 1809 and died October 7, 1849. An American writer, editor, and literary critic, Poe is best known for his poetry and short stories, particularly his tales of mystery and the macabre. He is widely regarded as a central figure of Romanticism in the United States and American literature as a whole, and he was one of the country's earliest writers of the short story format. Poe is generally considered the inventor of detective fiction and is credited with contributing to the emerging genre of science fiction. He was the first well-known American writer who tried to earn a living through writing alone which resulted in a financially difficult life and career.

Discover or research 5 more facts about the author or poem.

1 _____

_____

2 _____

_____

3 _____

_____

4 _____

_____

5 _____

_____

"My Boy" by Morris Rosenfeld

I have a little boy at home,
A pretty little son;
I think sometimes the world is mine
In him, my only one.

But seldom, seldom do I see
My child in heaven's light;
I find him always fast asleep...
I see him but at night.

Ere dawn my labor drives me forth;
'Tis night when I am free;
A stranger am I to my child;
And strange my child to me.

I come in darkness to my home,
With weariness and--pay;
My pallid wife, she waits to tell
The things he learned to say.

How plain and prettily he asked:
"Dear mamma, when's 'Tonight'?
O when will come my dear papa
And bring a penny bright?"

I hear her words--I hasten out--
This moment must it be!--
The father-love flames in my breast:
My child must look at me!

I stand beside the tiny cot,
And look, and list, and--ah!
A dream-thought moves the baby-lips:
"O, where is my papa!"

I kiss and kiss the shut blue eyes;
I kiss them not in vain.
They open,--O they see me then!
And straightway close again.

"Here's your papa, my precious one;--
A penny for you!"--ah!
A dream still moves the baby-lips:
"O, where is my papa!"

And I--I think in bitterness
And disappointment sore;
"Someday you will awake, my child,
To find me nevermore."

Analyze the Poem:

This poem is about a father who is not able to see his child during the day. It was written long ago and it's possible that the father worked from the very early morning to late into the evening to provide for his family. What might be other reasons he cannot see his child during the day? Use your imagination and include a reason why you think so.

1 _____

_____

2 _____

_____

3 _____

_____

4 _____

_____

5 _____

_____

We do know the author worked long hours in a tailor shop in New York. As a new immigrant, he worked very hard to help his family have a good life in America. Do you think it is right or fair for parents to work so hard but never have a chance to really be with their children? Why or why not?

_____

_____

_____

_____

_____

On the next page create a drawing next to the poem to help illustrate the story of the poem.

"My Boy"
by Morris Rosenfeld

I have a little boy at home,
A pretty little son;
I think sometimes the world is mine
In him, my only one.

But seldom, seldom do I see
My child in heaven's light;
I find him always fast asleep...
I see him but at night.

Ere dawn my labor drives me forth;
'Tis night when I am free;
A stranger am I to my child;
And strange my child to me.

I come in darkness to my home,
With weariness and--pay;
My pallid wife, she waits to tell
The things he learned to say.

How plain and prettily he asked:
"Dear mamma, when's 'Tonight'?
O when will come my dear papa
And bring a penny bright?"

I hear her words--I hasten out--
This moment must it be!--
The father-love flames in my breast:
My child must look at me!

I stand beside the tiny cot,
And look, and list, and--ah!
A dream-thought moves the baby-lips:
"O, where is my papa!"

I kiss and kiss the shut blue eyes;
I kiss them not in vain.
They open,--O they see me then!
And straightway close again.

"Here's your papa, my precious one;--
A penny for you!"--ah!
A dream still moves the baby-lips:
"O, where is my papa!"

And I--I think in bitterness
And disappointment sore;
"Someday you will awake, my child,
To find me nevermore."

Extended Exploration:

Write a short synopsis of the poem. What main idea or story was told?

_____

_____

_____

_____

_____

Morris Rosenfeld was born December 28, 1862 and died June 22, 1923 in New York City. He was a Yiddish poet. His work focused on the living circumstances of emigrants from Eastern Europe in New York's tailoring workshops. Maybe that explains the long working hours. He was the author of *Di Gloke* (*The Bell*) which included poems of a revolutionary character; later he bought and destroyed all copies of this book he could find. He wrote many books later, and his collected poems were published in 1904 under the title Gezamelte Lieder in New York.

Discover or research 5 more facts about the author or poem.

1 _____

_____

2 _____

_____

3 _____

_____

4 _____

_____

5 _____

_____

"Fairy Song" by Louisa May Alcott

The moonlight fades from flower and tree,
And the stars dim one by one;
The tale is told, the song is sung,
And the Fairy feast is done.
The night-wind rocks the sleeping flowers,
And sings to them, soft and low.
The early birds erelong will wake:
'T is time for the Elves to go.

O'er the sleeping earth we silently pass,
Unseen by mortal eye,
And send sweet dreams, as we lightly float
Through the quiet moonlit sky;--
For the stars' soft eyes alone may see,
And the flowers alone may know,
The feasts we hold, the tales we tell:
So 't is time for the Elves to go.

From bird, and blossom, and bee,
We learn the lessons they teach;
And seek, by kindly deeds, to win
A loving friend in each.
And though unseen on earth we dwell,
Sweet voices whisper low,
And gentle hearts most joyously greet
The Elves where'er they go.

When next we meet in the Fairy dell,
May the silver moon's soft light
Shine then on faces gay as now,
And Elfin hearts as light.
Now spread each wing, for the eastern sky
With sunlight soon will glow.
The morning star shall light us home:
Farewell! for the Elves must go.

Analyze the Poem:

This short poem has four stanzas. Write the main idea or story from each below.

1 _____

_____

2 _____

_____

3 _____

_____

4 _____

_____

This is a fairy tale or fantasy story. There seems to be a little lesson hidden inside the third stanza, "From bird, and blossom, and bee / We learn the lessons they teach / And seek, by kindly deeds, to win / A loving friend in each." What might be the author's message to us? Why do you think so?

_____
_____
_____
_____
_____
_____
_____

On the next page create a drawing around the text of the poem to help illustrate the meaning.

"Fairy Song"
by Louisa May Alcott

The moonlight fades from flower and tree,
And the stars dim one by one;
The tale is told, the song is sung,
And the Fairy feast is done.
The night-wind rocks the sleeping flowers,
And sings to them, soft and low.
The early birds erelong will wake:
'T is time for the Elves to go.

O'er the sleeping earth we silently pass,
Unseen by mortal eye,
And send sweet dreams, as we lightly float
Through the quiet moonlit sky;--
For the stars' soft eyes alone may see,
And the flowers alone may know,
The feasts we hold, the tales we tell:
So 't is time for the Elves to go.

From bird, and blossom, and bee,
We learn the lessons they teach;
And seek, by kindly deeds, to win
A loving friend in each.
And though unseen on earth we dwell,
Sweet voices whisper low,
And gentle hearts most joyously greet
The Elves where'er they go.

When next we meet in the Fairy dell,
May the silver moon's soft light
Shine then on faces gay as now,
And Elfin hearts as light.
Now spread each wing, for the eastern sky
With sunlight soon will glow.
The morning star shall light us home:
Farewell! for the Elves must go.

Extended Exploration:

Write a short synopsis of the poem. What main idea or story was told?

_____

_____

_____

_____

_____

Louisa May Alcott was born on November 29, 1832 and died March 6, 1888. She was an American novelist and poet best known as the author of the novel *Little Women* (1868) and its sequel *Little Men* (1871). She grew up among many of the well-known intellectuals of the day such as Ralph Waldo Emerson, Nathaniel Hawthorne, and Henry David Thoreau. Her family suffered severe financial difficulties and Alcott worked to help support the family from an early age. Early in her career, she sometimes used the pen name A. M. Barnard, under which she wrote novels for young adults.

Discover or research 5 more facts about the author or poem.

1 _____

_____

2 _____

_____

3 _____

_____

4 _____

_____

5 _____

_____

"The Ultimate Joy" by an unknown author

I have felt the thrill of passion in the poet's mystic book
And I've lingered in delight to catch the rhythm of the brook;
I've felt the ecstasy that comes when prima donnas reach
For upper C and hold it in a long, melodious screech.
And yet the charm of all these blissful memories fades away
As I think upon the fortune that befell the other day,
As I bring to recollection, with a joyous, wistful sigh,
That I woke and felt the need of extra covers in July.

Oh, eerie hour of drowsiness - 'twas like a fairy spell,
That respite from the terrors we have known, alas, so well,
The malevolent mosquito, with a limp and idle bill,
Hung supinely from the ceiling, all exhausted by his chill.
And the early morning sunbeam lost his customary leer
And brought a gracious greeting and a prophecy of cheer;
A generous affability reached up from earth to sky,
When I woke and felt the need of extra covers in July.

In every life there comes a time of happiness supreme,
When joy becomes reality and not a glittering dream.
'Tis less appreciated, but it's worth a great deal more
Than tides which taken at their flood lead on to fortune's shore.
How vain is Art's illusion, and how potent Nature's sway
When once in kindly mood she deigns to waft our woes away!
And the memory will cheer me, though all other pleasures fly,
Of how I woke and needed extra covers in July.

Analyze the Poem:

This short poem has three stanzas. Write the main idea from each below.

1 _____

_____

_____

2 _____

_____

_____

3 _____

_____

_____

What is the author's ultimate joy? How do you know?

_____

_____

_____

_____

_____

_____

_____

On the next page create a drawing around the text of the poem to help illustrate the meaning.

"The Ultimate Joy"
by an unknown author

I have felt the thrill of passion in the poet's mystic book
And I've lingered in delight to catch the rhythm of the brook;
I've felt the ecstasy that comes when prima donnas reach
For upper C and hold it in a long, melodious screech.
And yet the charm of all these blissful memories fades away
As I think upon the fortune that befell the other day,
As I bring to recollection, with a joyous, wistful sigh,
That I woke and felt the need of extra covers in July.

Oh, eerie hour of drowsiness - 'twas like a fairy spell,
That respite from the terrors we have known, alas, so well,
The malevolent mosquito, with a limp and idle bill,
Hung supinely from the ceiling, all exhausted by his chill.
And the early morning sunbeam lost his customary leer
And brought a gracious greeting and a prophecy of cheer;
A generous affability reached up from earth to sky,
When I woke and felt the need of extra covers in July.

In every life there comes a time of happiness supreme,
When joy becomes reality and not a glittering dream.
'Tis less appreciated, but it's worth a great deal more
Than tides which taken at their flood lead on to fortune's shore.
How vain is Art's illusion, and how potent Nature's sway
When once in kindly mood she deigns to waft our woes away!
And the memory will cheer me, though all other pleasures fly,
Of how I woke and needed extra covers in July.

Extended Exploration:

Write a short synopsis of the poem.

_____

_____

_____

_____

_____

The author of this poem is unknown. We may never know who wrote it but the message is clear and it is considered a popular poem. What would be your ultimate joy? Fame? Money? Love? Life?
Write your own rhyming poem below.

_____

_____

_____

_____

_____

_____

_____

"Marriage Fees" by an unknown author

The knot was tied; the pair were wed,
And then the smiling bridegroom said
Unto the preacher, "Shall I pay
To you the usual fee today.
Or would you have me wait a year
And give you then a hundred clear,
If I should find the marriage state
As happy as I estimate?"
The preacher lost no time in thought,
To his reply no study brought,
There were no wrinkles on his brow:
Said he, "I'll take three dollars now."

Analyze the Poem:

This poem about a wedding has a surprise, funny ending.
What is the "deal" the groom (husband) wants to make?

_____

_____

_____

_____

What does it mean when the poet writes of the preacher: "to his reply no study brought / There were no wrinkles on his brow:"?

_____

_____

_____

_____

The poem ends with the preacher saying he wants three dollars now rather than waiting a year for one hundred. Why is he not willing to wait for much more money?

_____

_____

_____

When you think about getting married, a very important occasion, making a bargain right before getting married is probably a bad idea. Why do you think it may have given the preacher an idea that the marriage might not be successful?

_____

_____

_____

Create a drawing on the next page based this poem. Draw around the poem.

"Marriage Fees"
by an unknown author

The knot was tied; the pair were wed,
And then the smiling bridegroom said
Unto the preacher, "Shall I pay
To you the usual fee today.
Or would you have me wait a year
And give you then a hundred clear,
If I should find the marriage state
As happy as I estimate?"
The preacher lost no time in thought,
To his reply no study brought,
There were no wrinkles on his brow:
Said he, "I'll take three dollars now."

Extended Exploration:

Write a short synopsis of the poem. What main idea or story was told?

_____

_____

_____

_____

_____

The author of this poem is unknown. We may never know who wrote it but the message is clear and it is considered a popular poem. Write your own funny poem about love using rhyming lines and include a funny ending.

_____

_____

_____

_____

_____

_____

_____

_____

"Two Fishers" by an unknown author

One morning when Spring was in her teens,
A morn to a poet's wishing,
All tinted in delicate pinks and greens,
Miss Bessie and I went fishing.

I in my rough and easy clothes,
With my face at the sun-tan's mercy;
She with her hat tipped down to her nose,
And her nose tipped, *vice versa*.

I with my rod, my reel, and my hooks,
And a hamper for lunching recesses;
She with the bait of her comely looks,
And the seine of her golden tresses.

So we sat us down on the sunny dike,
Where the white pond-lilies teeter,
And I went to fishing like quaint old Ike,
And she like Simon Peter.

All the noon I lay in the light of her eyes,
And dreamily watched and waited,
But the fish were cunning and would not rise,
And the baiter alone was baited.

And when the time of departure came,
My bag hung flat as a flounder;
But Bessie had neatly hooked her game,
A hundred-and-fifty-pounder.

Analyze the Poem:

This poem has six stanzas. Write the main idea or what you understand from each below.

1 _____

_____

2 _____

_____

3 _____

_____

4 _____

_____

5 _____

_____

6 _____

_____

In this poem there are two people fishing, but in the fifth stanza we see that the fish were smart *and would not rise*. This means they did not catch any fish. The last stanza says the boy's bag was flat, meaning empty, but Bessy did catch something. What did she catch and how do you know?

_____

_____

_____

_____

_____

On the back of this paper or a blank page create a drawing to help illustrate this poem. You may think of it as a whole or choose to focus on one part. Include some of the text in a creative way.

**Please visit www.FirehousePublications.com
for more educational resources by the author.**

- The Art Student's Workbook
- Elementary Art Workbook
- Art Assessments
- The Nearly Empty Coloring Book
- Artes Plásticas - Libro de Trabajo
- Chris & The Magic Shirt
- Art Camp - Creative Lessons for Children
- Art at the Heart - Exploring Core Content Through Art
- Sketchbook 101 & 102
- The Emotional Color Wheel
- The Interactive Sketchbook
- The Inspirational Sketchbook
- Sub Plans For Art Teachers
- If Picasso Went To The Zoo (English, Chinese, & Spanish)
- If Picasso Had a Christmas Tree
- If Picasso Went To The Sea
- If Picasso Went On Vacation

...And many more

Made in the USA
Middletown, DE
15 September 2017